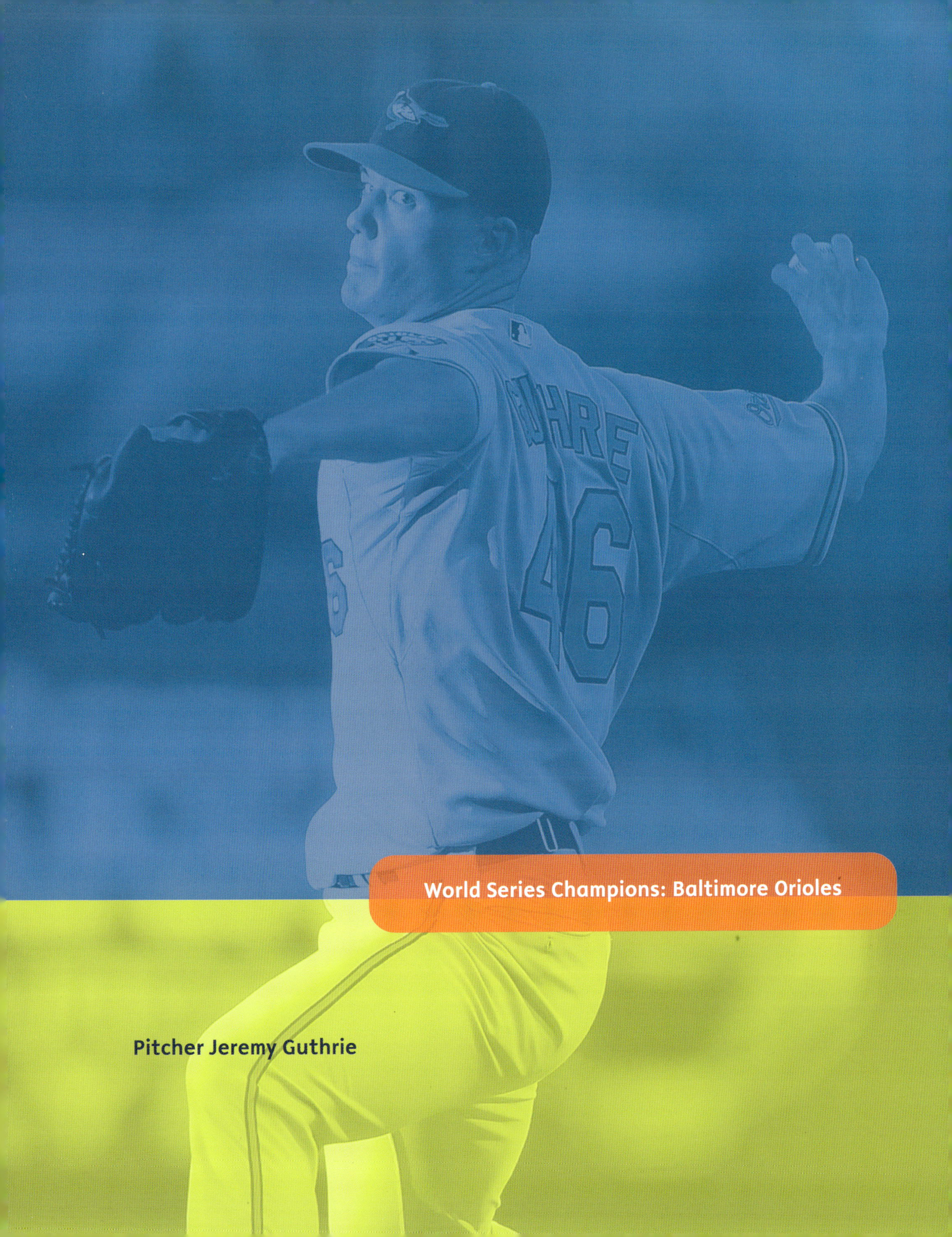

World Series Champions: Baltimore Orioles

Pitcher Jeremy Guthrie

First baseman Eddie Murray

WORLD SERIES CHAMPIONS

BALTIMORE ORIOLES

MICHAEL E. GOODMAN

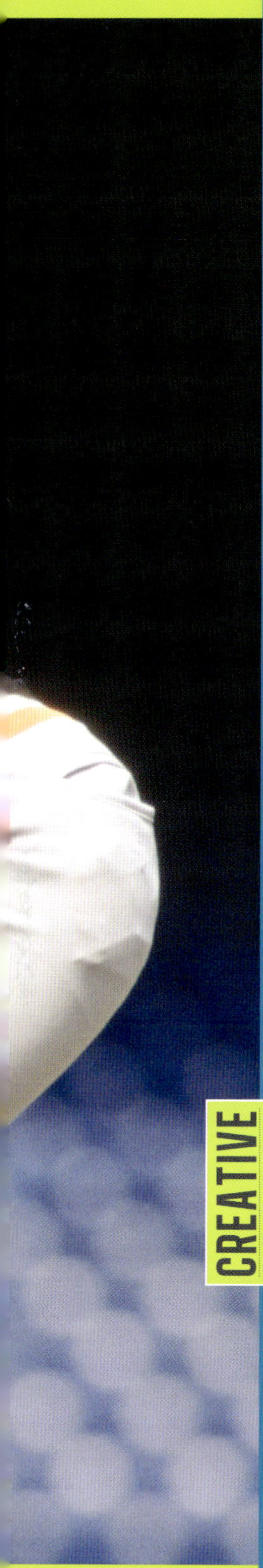

CREATIVE EDUCATION / CREATIVE PAPERBACKS

Published by Creative Education and Creative Paperbacks
P.O. Box 227, Mankato, Minnesota 56002
Creative Education and Creative Paperbacks are imprints of The Creative Company
www.thecreativecompany.us

Art Direction by Tom Morgan
Book production by Ciara Beitlich
Edited by Joe Tischler

Photographs by AP Images (Randy Litzinger/Icon Sportswire, Al Messerschmidt Archive), Getty (Bruce Bennett, Lisa Blumenfeld, Focus On Sport, Bob Gomel, Mitchell Layton, Ezra Shaw, Patrick Smith, The Sporting News, SPX/Diamond Images, Jamie Squire, Tony Tomsic, Ron Vesely), Shutterstock (Kevin Ruck)

Library of Congress Cataloging-in-Publication Data
Names: Goodman, Michael E., author.
Title: Baltimore Orioles / By Michael E. Goodman.
Description: Mankato, Minnesota : Creative Education / Creative Paperbacks, [2024] | Series: Creative sports: World Series champions | Includes index. | Audience: Ages 7-10 | Audience: Grades 2-3 | Summary: "Elementary-level text and engaging sports photos highlight the Baltimore Orioles' MLB World Series wins and losses, plus sensational players associated with the professional baseball team such as Jim Palmer."-- Provided by publisher.
Identifiers: LCCN 2023008171 (print) | LCCN 2023008172 (ebook) | ISBN 9781640268166 (library binding) | ISBN 9781682773666 (paperback) | ISBN 9781640009868 (pdf)
Subjects: LCSH: Baltimore Orioles (Baseball team)--History--Juvenile literature. | Baseball players--United States--Juvenile literature.
Classification: LCC GV875.B2 G66 2024 (print) | LCC GV875.B2 (ebook) | DDC 796.357/64097526--dc23/eng/20230224
LC record available at https://lccn.loc.gov/2023008171
LC ebook record available at https://lccn.loc.gov/2023008172

Printed in China

1970 World Series Champions

Shortstop Cal Ripken Jr.

CONTENTS

Home of the Orioles

Baltimore, Maryland, is the home of the first railroad line in the United States. One stop on that line was Camden Station. Today, a baseball **stadium** sits in that spot. It is called Oriole Park at Camden Yards. The Orioles baseball team plays there.

The Baltimore Orioles are a Major League Baseball (MLB) team. They play in the American League (AL) East Division. Their biggest **rivals** are the New York Yankees and Boston Red Sox. All MLB teams try to win the World Series to become champions.

Pitcher Mike Mussina

Naming the Orioles

The Baltimore Orioles got their name in 1954. Team owners picked the name Orioles after the state bird of Maryland. The feathers of male Baltimore orioles are bright orange and black. So, Orioles players wear orange and black hats. The caps have a cartoon oriole on them. Some fans call the team the "O's" or the "Birds."

Shortstop Vern Stephens

Orioles History

The Orioles began playing in 1901 in Milwaukee, Wisconsin. They were called the Brewers. The next year, the team moved to St. Louis, Missouri. Their name changed to Browns. The Browns usually finished near the bottom of the league. Finally, in 1944, All-Star shortstop Vern Stephens led them to their first World Series. They lost 4 games to 2.

In 1954, the Browns moved to Baltimore. They became the Orioles. Baltimore fans loved them. Two fan favorites were outfielder Frank Robinson and third baseman Brooks Robinson. In 1966, they led the Orioles to the World Series against the powerful Los Angeles Dodgers. Baltimore won all four games. They captured the championship!

Outfielder Frank Robinson

Pitcher Jim Palmer

In 1968, fiery manager Earl Weaver took over the team. He drove his players hard. They became big winners. The Orioles played in four World Series under Weaver. They won a championship in 1970. Top pitchers Jim Palmer and Dave McNally were hard to beat.

Future **Hall of Fame** players Cal Ripken Jr. and Eddie Murray led the O's to another **title** in 1983. Ripken was amazing. He played in every game for 15 seasons in a row!

Other Orioles Stars

Mike Mussina was one of the best pitchers in the 1990s. He played in five All-Star games.

Manager Buck Showalter took over in 2010. He led the Orioles to the **playoffs** three times. Sadly, they did not get to the World Series again.

Outfielder Cedric Mullins is one of the speediest runners in the AL. He twice stole at least 30 bases in a season.

Outfielder Cedric Mullins

Outfielder Anthony Santander

Right fielder Anthony Santander is a powerful batter. He also throws out many runners on the bases. Fans hope to see these stars play World Series games in Oriole Park soon.

About the Orioles

Started playing: 1901

League/division: American League, East Division

Team colors: black and orange

Home stadium: Oriole Park at Camden Yards

WORLD SERIES CHAMPIONSHIPS:

1966, 4 games to 0 over Los Angeles Dodgers

1970, 4 games to 1 over Cincinnati Reds

1983, 4 games to 1 over Philadelphia Phillies

Baltimore Orioles website: www.mlb.com/orioles

Glossary

Hall of Fame—a museum in which the best players of all time are honored

playoffs—games that the best teams play after a regular season to see who the champion will be

rival—a team that plays extra hard against another team

stadium—a building with tiers of seats for spectators

title—another word for championship

Third baseman Brooks Robinson

Index